my first visit to

the aquarium

English translation © Copyright 1990 by Barron's Educational Series, Inc.

© Parramón Ediciones, S.A.
First Edition, 1990
The title of the Spanish edition is *mi primera visita al acuario*

All inquiries should be addressed to:
Barron's Educational Series, Inc.
250 Wireless Boulevard
Hauppauge, New York 11788

Library of Congress Catalog Card No. 89-17986

International Standard Book No. 0-8120-4304-9

Library of Congress Cataloging-in-Publication Data

Parramón, José María.
    [Mi primera visita al acuario. English]
    My first visit to an aquarium / J.M. Parramón, G. Sales.—1st American ed.
      p. cm.
    Translation of: Mi primera visita al acuario.
    Summary; A class and its teacher visit an aquarium where they learn about
shellfish, reptiles, dolphins, sharks, and whales.
    ISBN 0-8120-4304-9
    1. Aquariums, Public—Juvenile literature. 2. Aquariums—Juvenile literature.
[1. Aquariums. 2. Marine animals.] I. Sales, G. II. Title.
QL78.P32713 1990   89-17986
591.92'0744—dc20   CIP
                                             AC

Printed in Spain

3456 9960 9876543

my first visit to
the aquarium

G. Sales
J.M. Parramón

BARRON'S

One day at school John, Mary, and Peter were looking at a book about life in the sea. "This is a whale," said the teacher.

The teacher explained, "The whale is a mammal. Most mammals—like dogs and cats and people—live on the land. But the whale is a mammal that lives in the sea. It is as big as a house. When a whale comes to the surface to breathe, it sprays a cloud of water droplets through its blowhole."

"And that's a shark," John exclaimed.

"Yes," said the teacher. "It is very dangerous because it is big and has huge teeth. It attacks and eats other fish. Sometimes it even attacks people who try to catch it with a harpoon."

"A huge octopus like this one could catch big fish, too," said Peter.

"But there are also small fish in the sea, aren't there?" asked John.

"Yes, and tomorrow we're going to see them at the aquarium," said the teacher.

"What a lot of fish!" the children said.
"And they come in so many different colors
and sizes!"

In one tank there were some small red fish with heads that looked like the head of a very small horse.

"Those are seahorses," explained the teacher.

In another tank, John, Peter, and Mary saw a lobster, some shrimps, some sea snails, and some scallops.

"Look, a giant tortoise, a swordfish, and an eel!" exclaimed Peter.

"The eel looks like a snake!" said Mary.

In another room the class saw glass compartments full of reptiles. In the first one there was a giant boa snake. The boa's body was almost as thick as the tree that it was coiled around.

Behind the glass of another compartment they saw a snake whose head was wider than its body.

The teacher explained, "That's a cobra. Its bite is very poisonous."

The small reptiles were much less frightening.

"These are lizards," explained the teacher.

"The green one on the rock looks like a snake with legs," said Mary.

Another lizard was catching a fly with its very long tongue.

"That's a chameleon," said the teacher. "Watch closely and you'll see it change its color."

Before leaving, the children went to the dolphin pool. The dolphins were having a marvelous time, swimming very fast and jumping in and out of the water.

Then they saw the dolphins jump up to take a fish from the trainer's hands. "That's fantastic!" said Peter.

"Yes," Mary agreed. "I'll never forget *my first visit to the aquarium!*"

MY FIRST VISIT TO THE AQUARIUM

Aquariums and Terrariums

There are two kinds of aquariums. One kind, used for keeping small, decorative fish, is the common water-filled glass container with sand, gravel, rocks, and marine plants on the bottom. A series of much larger tanks where many varieties of fish are kept is also called an aquarium. These *zoological aquariums* are often situated next to *terrariums*, which are places where reptiles and amphibians are raised, observed, and studied.

The best large aquariums include those in London, where the most exotic varieties of fish and crustaceans can be seen; New York, which has more than 5,000 tropical species; and Chicago, Naples, and Paris.

What Animals are Kept in Aquariums?

Zoological aquariums keep both large and small aquatic animals. For big marine animals like dolphins, whales, and other aquatic mammals there are special *oceanariums* where these animals have room to swim about.

At this point, children should be told that not all the animals in the aquarium or marine park are really fish. There are mollusks—like sea snails, clams, and scallops; there are crustaceans—like lobsters and shrimp; and there are cetacea—like the dolphins and whales. Despite appearances, the cetacea are really big mammals that live in the water and breathe using lungs (whereas fish use gills). Thus, all cetacea have to come to the surface regularly to take in air.

Because of their great intelligence and ability to send and analyze sounds under water, dolphins can be trained to perform amazing feats. Zoologists and marine park keepers often organize acrobatic shows where teams of dolphins jump in and out of the water and perform tricks on command, to the delight of young and old.

The Purpose of Big Aquariums

The purpose of zoological aquariums and terrariums is to conserve aquatic and land animals for the observation and study of their habits. Scientists can thus discover the ecological laws determining the behavior of the various species, always taking into account that the biological responses of animals in captivity will of course be slightly different from those of animals living in their natural environment. Aquariums also help children and interested adults observe and learn about exotic species from distant countries.

Domestic Aquariums

Domestic aquariums are water-filled containers that are used to keep live aquatic animals and plants. They vary in size from single fish bowls to large, elaborate tanks. But in any case, like zoological aquariums, they must reproduce the living conditions found in nature if the inhabitants are to survive.

How to Make Your Own Aquarium

The general directions for making your own aquarium are not very complicated. First you need a glass or plastic container with transparent sides. At the bottom, put a layer of sand 1 inch (25 mm) thick. Then put in a sheet of plastic that will stop the sand from moving when you fill the aquarium with water. Once you have put in the water, you can take out the plastic. Plants and rocks, which can be purchased at specialized stores, can be introduced immediately. However, it is best to wait about a week before putting in the fish. This gives the plants time to establish themselves before the fish start to brush against them or bite them. A small air compressor is needed to increase the amount of oxygen in the water, and a filter is needed to keep the water clean. It is also necessary to control the lighting, the temperature, and (in a salt water tank) the salinity of the water. Experts in the shops will help you choose species that can be kept together. They will also advise you about the accessories needed to obtain the proper environment for your particular selection.

It can be extremely gratifying to have an aquarium at home. Its decorative value is complemented by the relaxing effect of watching fish swimming serenely about the water. Children can also find the responsibility of looking after an aquarium highly rewarding and educational.